Subprime Mortgage Crisis
An Introduction

:: Author ::

Vaishaliben Makwana

Assistant Professor
Government Arts & Commerce College, Kathlal

PUBLISHED BY

Hemchandracharya International Publishing House
HQ. At & Po. Chaveli., Ta- Chansma,
Dist- Patan, North Gujarat, India, Asia.
www.iphouseindia.com

First Publication: 1ˢᵗ June, 2015

Copyright: Author
(c) **Vaishaliben Makwana**

ISBN:- 978-1-51747-709-7

Price: Rs.800/- INDIA
$ 15 OUTSIDE INDIA

PUBLISHED BY

Hemchandracharya International Publishing House
HQ. At & Po. Chaveli., Ta- Chansma,
Dist- Patan, North Gujarat, India, Asia.
www.iphouseindia.com

Dedicated
to
my
Parents

Subprime Mortgage Crisis: An Introduction

As Safe As Houses!

"As safe as houses", this phrase is often used in our society. A house is supposed to be the safest place than one can be. Also, until 2008, most Americans and also most people worldwide considered this to be true of investments. A house was about as safe as an investment can get. It used to have a steady compounding rate of appreciation. The growth was nothing spectacular, rather just safe and sound cash flows that came in like clockwork.

True, that the average person had heard about housing market booms in some distant past. However, almost no-one had seen or experienced one very recently. Hence, although stocks, bonds and other investments being traded on the market were viewed as risky, a house was a different matter altogether.

This was about to change in 2008, with the bust of subprime mortgage crisis. The market may not have realized it. However, the houses were not safe at all. It turns out that the houses were built and sold on the basis of some very dubious lending practices. This is the reason why the study of subprime mortgage crisis is necessary for anyone studying asset bubbles.

Magnitude of the Crisis

United States and the world may have seen many housing crashes. However subprime mortgage crisis was distinctly different on many counts.

Firstly, it was the biggest bust of any kind that the world had seen since the Great Depression of 1929. This places in the category of the worst financial events that the world has ever witnessed.

Secondly, the crisis did not stay local to the United States. The subprime mortgage crisis became a worldwide phenomenon. Hence falling housing prices and rising delinquencies in the US became the cause for a worldwide recession and slowdown.

Thirdly, the crisis did not stay concentrated to the housing or banking sector. Rather, the crisis became an underlying economic current which caused bankruptcies of major corporations worldwide even though these corporations had absolutely nothing to do with mortgages or housing!

Ever since, the subprime mortgage crisis is used as a case study, a reminder of how interconnected our global financial system really has become.

Effects

The effects of the subprime mortgage crisis were too many to be listed down in this discussion. We shall have a detailed look at them in the module. However, just to provide a glimpse, this catastrophic event led to changes in the following areas:

- **Banking:** The subprime mortgage crisis has shaped the public opinion that banks are indeed working against the general benefit rather than for it. Many people had to lose their homes, suffer job loss and many such economic calamities unfolded because of what is perceived as a wrongdoing of banks built on their greed. Hence increasing public clamor against the perceived corruption of the banks led to increased regulation for the banking industry. Also the industry underwent severe change as some of the big players simply went bankrupt in the wake of the crisis. Mergers and acquisitions were rampant. If one looks at the banking industry in 2010, the big players are completely different from those in 2005.

- **Financial Markets:** The subprime mortgage crisis had a catastrophic effect on the financial markets around the world. Most indices lost their value by as much as 50% during the crisis. Stock markets were the worst hit and so were derivative markets. Also, as mentioned earlier this was not a local phenomenon. The tanking of stock indices was happening simultaneously in London, Tokyo, Hong Kong, New York, Singapore and any other major financial center in the world causing an atmosphere of unprecedented panic throughout the world.

- **Political:** Not surprisingly, a major financial event also turned out to be a major political event in the United States. The Republican government started being viewed as extremely pro crony capitalism and silently vetoing corruption. As a result, the

Democrats and more specifically Barack Obama was catapulted to power. A lot of political programs were created with the intent to clean up the mess caused by the crisis. Also, a lot of money was spent on public welfare to ensure that people reeling from the effects of this catastrophe do find at least the basic necessities of life available.

- **Main Street:** The subprime mortgage crisis made life of the common man miserable. There was a high degree of resentment and the "Wall Street vs. Main Street" theme became common all over the media. There was increasing unemployment caused by the double whammy of recession and outsourcing. Also, with interest rates rising, the economy was on the verge of deflation. Consumer spending and consumer confidence index was at an all time low. This was one of the worst financial periods in history of the United States.

Raging Debates

The subprime mortgage crisis led to a lot of debates. Talk shows and newspaper columns were full of debates. Blame was being shifted from one group of stakeholders to the other. There were multiple hypotheses as to what caused this catastrophe. The government was forced to act on these theories and some pieces of legislation were passed or removed to make the financial system more stable.

Throughout the course of this module we will look at some of the most prominent theories and debates and make an attempt to analyze them.

Dot Com Bust: Starting Point of Subprime Mortgage Crisis

The subprime mortgage crisis is a unique case in the fact that this bubble started from an earlier present bubble in the United States. Many critics argue that the policies enacted by the government to minimize the pain of the aftermath of the dot com bubble burst of the late nineties is the chief cause of the subprime mortgage crisis.

The dot com bubble was a bubble which flourished in the nineties. The internet was an extremely new business and many companies that had leveraged the internet were having multibillion dollar valuations. There came a time when investors were so euphoric about dot com companies that any company could add millions of dollars to its market capitalization by simply adding dot com to its name.

During the late nineties and the first few years of the new millennium, the US economy was constantly hit by adverse events. Some of them were as follows:

- **Dot Com Bust:** The dot com bust happened sometime in 2001. Investors woke up to the fact that not every company that operates via the internet is going to turn in millions of dollars in profits. They also realized that in the process of acquiring more and more of these dot com companies, they might have inadvertently pushed up the stock prices beyond sustainable limits. Soon came a massive sell off and the United States stock markets were reeling. This created a lack of consumer confidence and consumer spending.

- **Enron Scandal:** To make matters worse, the biggest corporate fraud in the history of America also unfolded at about the same time. Enron, had been swindling billions of dollars of shareholders money. It had also played with the life savings of thousands of employees. This fraud also came to light in 2001 and the company was declared bankrupt. Enron had been a Fortune 100 company and employed thousands of people. Enron's bankruptcy plunged the economy into a crisis negatively affecting consumer confidence and consumer spending.

- **Hurricane Katrina:** The grave natural disaster of hurricane Katrina also struck New Orleans at around the same time. Once again there was large scale destruction of life and property having adverse effects on the United States economy.

- **Terrorist Attacks:** To add up to all this, the United States was further struck by a terrorist attack on the 11th September 2001. This plunged the nation into war. An overseas war means huge expenses and also huge debt. This also created ripple effects in the economy and there was a loss of consumer confidence.

Low Interest Rates

The United States government was reeling from successive economic blows. The Federal Reserve i.e. the central bank of the United States had to come up with a way to help expand the economy. As a result they resorted to cutting interest rates. Within a two year period, interest rates were cut from 5.75% to 1.25%. This dramatic fall did not happen in a single interest rate cut. Rather a series of interest rate cuts were introduced whenever the monetary policy was announced. These rates were historically very low for the United States and the inflation rate was greater than these interest rates meaning that the real interest rate was negative. The situation was left this way for a few years.

To many observers and critics, this was the death knell. This is what they believe resulted in the subprime mortgage crisis.

Speculative Housing Market Activity

The government did succeed in its goal of increasing spending and reducing monetary turmoil by resorting to interest rate cuts. However, this resulted in speculative activity in the housing market. The details of the same have been outlined below.

- **Housing Prices:** The housing prices in the United States doubled during the period when interest rates were low. That was a 14% year on year return on the housing prices. Historically, the housing prices in the United States moved at around the rate of inflation. This housing boom was fueled by the sudden availability of a massive amount of credit in the markets. Hence, this could be considered as one of the prime causes of the subprime mortgage crisis.

- **Lending Requirements:** With the availability of excess money, banks were also forced to lower their lending standards and make unsustainable loans. There was just too much money in the market and banks had to compete to lend that money.

- **Mal Investments:** The housing boom was indeed a bubble because most of the houses that were sold were not inhabited by people. About 40% of the houses sold during the period were vacation homes. Then, again another 22% were being flipped over and over again by speculators looking to make a quick buck. The actual need i.e. the number of houses where people actually stayed were very less. It was just the easy availability of mortgages to pretty much anybody that pushed the banks into making mal-investments.

The Seeds Were Sown

At the time of the boom, housing prices seemed to be rising. Anybody who was investing ended up making money and all seemed fine. However, it is during this period and because of the low interest rates introduced by the Fed that the seeds of a catastrophe were sown. The subprime mortgage crisis was thus in a way the offshoot of an attempt to avoid the dot com bubble bust.

Political Incentive for Home Ownership

I

If we were to read any newspaper articles or access any media reports post the subprime mortgage debacle, we were sure to find the banks and other corporations being blamed. Corporate greed was the highlighted fact in this financial catastrophe. However, there was a neglected aspect too. Many commentators have believed that corporate greed was not the starting point of this crisis. Instead, the starting point was based on political motives. In simple words, that is to say that the government is as responsible for the subprime crisis as the banks were, if not more!

Let's explore this point of view and the debate surrounding it in this discussion.

Community Reinvestment Act

The center point of the case against the government has been a legislation called the Community Reinvestment Act. This legislation was not new in the nineties or early 2000's. Rather it was enacted by President Jimmy Carter in 1997. However, until Bill Clinton's regime, it was like a toothless tiger. Bill Clinton's government made drastic changes to this act. Many commentators believe that these changes were what ended up in the disaster a few years later. Let's have a closer look at the Community Reinvestment Act

- **Alleged Discrimination:** There were allegations from many political leaders that banks were "redlining" certain neighborhoods. Redlining meant drawing an imaginary line around certain neighborhoods and refusing to grant loans and other financial services to the residents who stayed there. Most of these neighborhoods were inhabited by minorities like African Americans and Hispanics. Therefore, there was a widely held belief that the "White" people in charge of the banks were doing this redlining on purpose to keep the minorities oppressed.

  Banks have reacted to this allegation by denying it vehemently. They stated that their lending practices did not have any ulterior racial motives. They were lending more and more to minorities such as Asian

Americans and Indian Americans. Banks expressed their concern over the crime rates and lifestyle in these neighborhoods. They were of the opinion that lending to the residents of these neighborhoods regardless of their race was a risky proposition. Hence the redlining which was meant to justify the increased risk.

- **Lower Lending Standards:** The banks arguments did not go down too well with the government. The government looked at some statistics which stated that while 89% of the loan applications were approved for "white" borrowers there acceptance rate was only 72% for the minorities such as African Americans and Hispanics. Therefore the government ordered the banks to lower their lending standards as a part of incorporating the minorities more into the financial system.

One of the biggest issues surrounding this debate was the fact that many African Americans and Hispanics did not have a regular job. Therefore there was no job history to verify and mitigate the risks. Documents such as salary slips were not available for many of these people. The government therefore ordered the banks to accept self verified statements of income from these borrowers and make loans accordingly! This practice was under heavy criticism later when the crisis unfolded and lower lending standards were blamed.

- **Norms to be Met:** The government's directions on this lending were legally binding. Banks were subject to regular audits regarding the race of the borrowers they lend to. A certain minimum percentage had to be from the minority community. If these standards were not met, banks were penalized monetarily and the growth of their branches was stalled. Hence, banks had no option but to comply with these lending standards.

Underwriting Bodies

The government interference with bank lending did not stop with the Community Reinvestment Act. They had created three special quasi government agencies called

Freddie Mac, Fannie Mae and Ginnie Mae. The job of these agencies was to buy loans from the commercial and trust banks and then securitize them. These agencies played a huge part in the crisis and left the taxpayers' pockets short by billions of dollars. However, we will discuss that in detail in the next couple of discussions.

Debate

When the subprime mortgage crisis actually occurred, there was wide spread debate about the true cause. When Community Reinvestment Act was brought into question, some of the proponents of this act, particularly the minorities reacted by vehemently lashing out facts. A couple of them are as follows:

- **Commercial Loans:** A big chunk of the loans that went bad were subprime commercial mortgage loans. This means they were used to finance commercial real estate and not residential which was under the purview of the Communities Reinvestment Act. Hence, they believed that the banks were making false accusations and deflecting blame since the government never forced them to make bad commercial loans!

- **Statistically Invalid:** Also, minority leader pointed out to the lack of statistical evidence to back up the claims being made against the legislation. They stated that the rates of delinquency amongst minority borrowers were only 6% higher than the "Whites" and hence the blame cannot be laid on the act. A wide variety of such statistics were exchanged back and forth. However, nothing has been conclusively proven.

Conclusion

The United States government had made home ownership a highly politicized agenda. The government was literally forcing people to buy homes and made home ownership a measurable fact which was used by leaders in their election campaign.

Well, it cannot be proven with facts that such government policies were indeed responsible for the crisis. However, it definitely raises a question? Is it the government's job to assist people in obtaining houses? Or is it an issue best left to the markets?

The Case Of Freddie Mac, Fannie Mae and Ginnie Mae

The role that the government played in causing the subprime mortgage crisis is highly debatable. However, the same cannot be said regarding the role performed by the so called government sponsored entities.

The Federal Home Loan Mortgage Corporation (Freddie Mac), Federal National Mortgage Association (Fannie Mae) and Government National Mortgage Association (Ginnie Mae) are three such entities. The newspapers, media and even the general population were of the opinion that these corporations have caused mayhem in the mortgage markets. In the aftermath of the subprime mortgage crisis, these agencies required the highest bailout financed by taxpayers dollars.

These agencies were created many years before the crisis. The reason behind their foundation was to make home ownership more affordable in the United States.

These agencies were formed to create a secondary mortgage market meant to provide liquidity to the originators of residential mortgages. These agencies were empowered as and when the political motives behind Community Reinvestment Act became strong. In this discussion and the next we will study in detail, the workings and shortcomings of these agencies.

Government Sponsored Entities

Freddie Mac, Fannie Man and Ginnie Mae were all government sponsored entities. The average person may not even know the meaning of these words. A government sponsored entity is a weird combination between a government entity and a corporate entity. Hence it is often known as a quasi-government entity.

This means that these agencies were created because a special legislation was passed by the US Congress for each of their creation. Therefore, they got a charter from the government. However, they are also publically listed corporations which trade on the market! Hence, they are both public and private at the same time which confuses a lot of people.

Government Control

Freddie Mac, Fannie Man and Ginnie Mae are also subject to a lot of control from the government. At least this was supposed to be theoretically the case. Some of the restrictions levied are as follows:

- The government has the authority to appoint five of the 18 board members in these coporations. Hence, theoretically, the management of these firms is controlled by the governments.

- Freddie Mac, Fannie Man and Ginnie Mae are not allowed to participate in the primary mortgage markets. This means that they cannot directly make any loans to the borrowers. They have to form the secondary mortgage markets leaving the task of loan origination to commercial and trust banks.

- Freddie Mac, Fannie Man and Ginnie Mae are also subject to limits which govern the maximum size of the mortgages that they buy. This size is linked to the housing price index. This is done to ensure that these quasi government agencies are actually buying the mortgages that help the lower and middle income groups rather than financing the wealthy households.

- These agencies are also subject to regulations which govern the quality of mortgages that they can purchase from the open market. The rules stated that Freddie Mac, Fannie Man and Ginnie Mae can only buy a mortgage if the borrower has put in at least 20% of the margin money or the mortgage is guaranteed by an external credit enhancement like insurance. However, later these rules were circumvented by these agencies.

- Freddie Mac, Fannie Man and Ginnie Mae are also subject to regulatory checks just like commercial and trust banks. These audits are conducted at periodic intervals.

It is for this reason that the bonds sold by these quasi government agencies were not listed either under government or private bonds. Rather, a special new section called "government sponsored agencies" was created to list them.

Monopoly

Freddie Mac, Fannie Man and Ginnie Mae were started in the 1970's. They really started to pick some traction by the 1990's. These agencies had a first mover advantage in the secondary mortgage markets section. This coupled with the fact that they had major advantages by being a quasi government entity created a virtual monopoly of these agencies.

Freddie Mac, Fannie Man and Ginnie Mae have held more than 90% of the secondary mortgage market for decades ever since their inception. It was only in the late 1990's and early 2000's that Wall Street investment banks also wanted a piece of the secondary mortgage pie.

This is when they took advantage of the limitations present in the charter of Freddie Mac, Fannie Man and Ginnie Mae. They started buying mortgages which were greater in value than those which these agencies were allowed to buy. They also started buying mortgages which were more riskier i.e. did not meet the minimum down payment criteria or did not have an external credit enhancement.

Once the Wall Street took to buying such riskier loans, they started getting more and more share of the security mortgage markets. Seeing their market share erode Freddie Mac, Fannie Man and Ginnie Mae also started buying riskier mortgages by finding ways to circumvent the laws.

These riskier mortgages were what later caused the subprime mortgage crisis. Since both Wall Street banks as well as government agencies were aggressively buying and selling these mortgages, both of them found themselves close to bankruptcy when the market went bust and both of them were later bailed out with taxpayer dollars. The story of how that unfolded will be covered in later modules.

Advantages to Freddie Mac, Fannie Man and Ginnie Mae

In the previous discussion, we covered the history and the roots of special government agencies called Freddie Mac, Fannie Man and Ginnie Mae. We understood that these organizations are hybrid in nature and that their stock is sold on the stock exchange whereas at the same time, they have a government charter! The exact nature of these organizations is subject to a lot of debate.

The foremost question that arises is that the stockholders of a government company will obviously have some major advantages over their private counterparts. In the case of Freddie Mac, Fannie Man and Ginnie Mae this was most likely true. In this discussion, we will cover this question in detail. **Let's have a look at some of the special advantages that were conferred upon Freddie Mac, Fannie Man and Ginnie Mae.**

Implicit Guarantee

The market had a collective belief that agencies like Freddie Mac, Fannie Man and Ginnie Mae cannot fail. This is because they are partly the creation of the government. This belief also turned out to be true. When the crisis finally broke out in 2008, the first people to receive help were these government agencies.

The Federal Government had provided billions of dollars in lines of credit to these agencies as a part of their charter. Hence, even in a non crisis situation, these agencies could simply borrow money from the government. When the crisis did break out, the government was forced to extend these credit lines by many more billions and immediately rescue Freddie Mac, Fannie Man and Ginnie Mae.

This is because the market bought these loans on the assumption that the US government and the US taxpayers were implicitly backing them. A failure on the part of Freddie Mac, Fannie Man and Ginnie Mae to repay their loans would imply a failure of the United States government and that would be the beginning of a world-wide catastrophe.

Agency Bonds

As we can see from the above point that the securities sold by Freddie Mac, Fannie Man and Ginnie Mae were relatively risk free. Hence if you were a lender in the bond market, lending money to these agencies would also be considered relatively risk free because there was an implicit backing of the US government.

It is for this reason that the bonds issues by these agencies to raise money were issued at a lower rate of interest than the private parties. There were three categories of bonds in the market i.e. the government bonds, the private bonds and a brand new category called the agency bonds which reflected the higher than government but lower than private risk of these agencies.

Freddie Mac, Fannie Man and Ginnie Mae got an advantage of 25 to 40 basis points in the bond market. This is a huge advantage when it comes to consistently borrowing billions of dollars. Hence, many critics argue that these agencies had special powers in their charter which enabled them to grow beyond their size and later cause catastrophic default.

Higher Yields

Freddie Mac, Fannie Man and Ginnie Mae had lower borrowing rates. This meant that they could lend at higher rates and then always make a risk free profit.

This would be outrageous since the government would have created a private entity that is guaranteed profits by government charter!

While many critics argue that this was indeed the case, the government, Freddie Mac, Fannie Man and Ginnie Mae all deny these allegations vehemently. The governments side of the story is that 75% of the savings accrued as a result of lower lending rates to these agencies were passed on to the borrowers. There have been several statistics published to justify this claim.

However, everyone familiar with the issue and not having any vested interests will agree that Freddie Mac, Fannie Man and Ginnie Mae indeed had special privileges

Exempt From State and Local Taxes

One of the biggest privileges that were bestowed upon Freddie Mac, Fannie Man and Ginnie Mae was the fact that they were exempt from state and local taxes. Since they were government bodies chartered by federal law, they were not under the purview of state and local tax agencies. Hence, while their competitors had to pay state and local taxes and increase their input costs, Freddie Mac, Fannie Man and Ginnie Mae had no such compulsion!

When you add together low interest rates and tax exemption, the picture of why these agencies held a monopoly over the secondary mortgage market became clear.

Exempt From Regulations

Lastly, Freddie Mac, Fannie Man and Ginnie Mae were not subject to the same regulations as commercial banks or investment banks. In the US, banking had been a highly regulated industry and complying with the regulations cost a lot of money, time and severely restrict the ability of an organization to engage in trade.

Freddie Mac, Fannie Man and Ginnie Mae did not face these limitations to the full. Sure, there was regulation of these quasi government agencies as well. However, it was nowhere as stringent as those imposed on the banks.

To sum it all up, **Freddie Mac, Fannie Man and Ginnie Mae had major advantages over their**

competitors. These advantages were no earned in the open market rather they were simply bestowed upon them by the government. Hence, later when tax payer dollars were used to pay up the bill of an already over privileged corporation, there was a massive hue and cry.

Types of Mortgages

The United States mortgage market was considered one of the most advanced markets in the world. It seemed like the lenders there had figured out the alchemy of finance. It seemed like they had figured out a way to make the risks go away. A traditional market would have only a single type of mortgage. However, nontraditional markets such as United States had a wide variety of mortgages. Let's have a closer look at the types of these mortgages in this as well as the next couple of discussions.

In this discussion we will focus on types of mortgages from the lenders point of view. We will look at the pros and cons from a lenders point of view:

Prime Loans

Prime loans were the traditional category loans. This meant that they were given to borrowers which could fulfill all the requirements i.e. they had a proper job, not much debt, had all their documents in place and had a good credit score. Also, these borrowers had enoush funds to put a decent amount of margin money into the loan account.

These borrowers would qualify for a mortgage under the most stringent standards. These are the people that would have got a mortgage 40 years prior to the subprime crisis when all the financial innovation was not present. Since these borrowers represent the least risk, these were called prime borrowers and the loans granted to them would be called as prime loans. Quasi federal agencies like Freddie Mac, Fannie Man and Ginnie Mae were allowed to purchase their loans from the lenders and then securitize them. Hence, the very low risk that these borrowers represented made them eligible for a very low interest rate called the prime interest rate.

A-Minus Loans

The first category of loans with financial innovation is called A minus loans. These loans are granted to borrowers who may not have a good credit score. In this case a good credit score is defined as a credit score below 680. These borrowers usually have filed for foreclosures, bankruptcies, write-offs or such other unfavorable financial decisions in the recent past. This reduces their credit scores and hence they do not qualify for a mortgage.

However, lenders in the United States were of the view that loans could and should be made to these borrowers too! For this purpose, they increased the interest rate to offset the additional risk of default on these loans and started offering mortgages to these slightly delinquent buyers. However, these mortgages were risky and hence agencies like Freddie Mac, Fannie Man and Ginnie Mae would not purchase them in the secondary mortgage market. This changed when Wall Street investment banks started buying them from the secondary market. A minus loans formed one of the largest categories of loans that were securitized. Also A minus loans were at the heart of the crisis when the loans started defaulting.

Alt-A Loans

A lower category of loans which are offered in the market were called Alt-A loans. These loans were very similar to A minus loans. In fact the similarity was so striking that some lenders would classify Alt A and A minus in the same category. However, there was a difference. Alt-A loans were given out to borrowers with insufficient documentation. This meant that they were given to people who did not have a regular job or business but on the other hand had sporadic or unconventional employment. They may or may not have a credit score less than 680. The lack of documents made them Alt A borrowers.

Once again the lenders charged a higher interest rate to reflect the higher risk of these loans. Once again the quasi federal agencies like Freddie Mac, Fannie Man and Ginnie Mae would not purchase these loans from the secondary mortgage market. However, Wall Street investment banks used a variety of credit enhancement techniques to make these loans marketable in the securities market. At the height of the subprime boom, Alt-A loans were amongst the most popular.

Subprime Loans

The next category of loans was given out to borrowers who had a bad credit history. These loans were made to borrowers who in the past had a track record of being unable to meet repayment schedules. These were people who had borrowed excessively often to the point of default. They were always a few months behind on their payment schedules and under normal circumstances these people would simply be denied loans.

These borrowers did not have any assets that could be used as collateral. Also they did not have enough money to make margin payments on the mortgage. In many cases, their houses were financed for more than 100% to allow them to meet the legal expenses as well as the expenses of moving into the house. These individuals could not possibly make the mortgage payments and maintain their living expenses from their known income.

Since these loans were on the verge of bankruptcy the moment they were made, these loans had a very high interest rate referred to as the subprime mortgage rate. These loans were purchased by investment bankers when the used the technique called "tranching" which will be explained in a later discussion. Federal agencies like Freddie Mac, Fannie Man and Ginnie Mae stayed away from these loans even at the height of the borrowing boom since their charter simply did not allow them to meddle with such loans.

Second Mortgages

In traditional lending environments, there is usually a single mortgage for every house. However, this was not the case during the borrowing boom. If a person had significantly more equity in the house i.e. the house was worth a lot more than the money owed on it, then the person could also take a second mortgage.

The second mortgage would usually be from a different lender and would be financed at a higher rate. The higher rate would reflect the additional risk that the second lender is taking by accepting being paid down only after the first lender is paid in full in the event of a default. Having two to three mortgages was common in the United States during the peak of the borrowing boom. Federal agencies such as Freddie Mac, Fannie Man and Ginnie Mae usually stayed away from these loans in the secondary mortgage markets. Once again these loans were consumed by Wall Street using the tranching technique.

Hence a lender during the borrowing boom had significant options to make loans. The types of loans stated above include pretty much every requirement of the borrower regardless of whether it would be sound lending practice to make these loans.

At that point in time, it was hailed as a financial innovation. However, when we look at it today, it seems like a house of cards built on a shaky foundation waiting to collapse and that was happened in the end.

Types of Mortgages from Borrower's Point of View

In the previous discussion, we studied about the different types of loans from the lenders point of view. Therefore we looked at the classification of the loans based on the types of borrowers. **In this discussion we will look at the different types of loans from the borrower's point of view**. Since the US mortgage market was highly diversified, borrowers had innumerable options to choose from. This discussion provides an indicative list. The following are the most common types of loans.

Amortized Loans

The regular types of mortgage loans that are made worldwide are called amortization loans. This is because these loans follow a financial procedure called amortization. **Amortization means principal and interest payments are being made simultaneously in a monthly payment**. The amount of the monthly payment remains the same i.e. it is an annuity.

However, the monthly payment has two parts interest and principal. In the beginning of the loan the interest payments are highest. This is because the outstanding principal is highest. However, during the tenure of the loan as more and more principal is paid back the interest component reduces and more money starts going towards the principal repayment. During the last few payments, almost the entire payment consists of principal as there is hardly any interest left to pay. These loans are the most regular types of loans and carry the minimal risk from the lenders point of view. This is the most conservative type of lending.

Interest Only Loans

The interest only loans are the exact opposite of amortized loans. These loans do not follow the amortization procedure. In this case, the borrower is only expected to make monthly interest payments. Since these are no principal payments being made, the amount of principal does not reduce and the interest outstanding remains the same each month. Let's understand this with the help of an example.

In case a borrower was to borrow $100 in an interest only mortgage at a 0.25% per month interest only loan, they were liable to pay only 25 cents every month. However, the interest will remain constant at 25 cents until the rates change. Also, the principal will remain constant at $100. Even if the borrower paid the mortgage payments for 20 years there would still be the $100 principal outstanding. Since the principal is never paid off, and the value of the house may fluctuate in value, these types of loans are considered very risky from the lenders point of view. A borrower may suddenly go underwater if a mortgage is structured this way and that is what happened in the subprime mortgage crisis. The interest rates on these types of loans are generally higher than the interest rates on amortized loans.

Also, these loans are largely used by speculators i.e. people who have no interest in moving into the house. Rather they just want to keep paying interest till as long as they hold their investment.

Bullet Payment Loans

The third type of loan from the borrower's point of view is the bullet payment loan. In many ways it is a hybrid between the earlier two types of loans. The bullet payment loan is like the interest only loan in the sense that the borrower only has to make monthly interest payments. However, it is also like the amortization loan in the sense that the borrower has to make principal payments at certain specified intervals. Let's understand this with the help of an example.

So if a borrower takes a $100 bullet mortgage loan with a 0.25% monthly interest, then the borrower has to pay 25 cents every month for the interest payments. Then, they also have to pay $10.25 in the 12th month (or any month agreed upon). Here $10 will go towards principal payments whereas 25 cents will go towards interest payments.

Once again, these loans were largely used by speculators who did not intend to hold on the property till the bullet payment came due.

Piggyback Loans: Piggyback loans were the start of deteriorating lending standards. These loans were basically meant to cover the mortgage margin payments. Quasi-Government agencies like Freddie Mac and Fannie Mae required that the borrowers finance at least 20% of the loan value. Hence, banks started lending them this 20% in the form of piggyback loans. This was a separate loan account. The borrower would then use this money to pay the margin money and the resultant loan could then be sold off in the secondary mortgage markets to these quasi government agencies. This was a way of circumventing the regulation. In essence the borrower had put no money down but it appeared as though they had put 20% margin payments.

No Documentation: Lenders in the midst of a borrowing boom were finding it hard to find enough people to give money to. It is for this reason that they had to relax the conventional mortgage lending norms. Conventional mortgage lending relied extensively on paperwork. Documents were required to ascertain the net worth of the individual as well as their projected cash flows. In the midst of the lending mania, lenders decided to ignore all of this. Loans were given out to people who did not have regular jobs or income documents. Instead, people could just self verify their income and the documents would be considered to be good enough for the bank's purposes.

Ninja Loans: Perhaps the most outrageous type of loan during the subprime mortgage crisis was the NINJA loan. NINJA stands for No Income, No Jobs and No Assets. Conventional lending would have frowned upon such an application for thousands of dollars worth mortgage loans. However, new age lenders decided that they were actually lending against a security i.e. a house and therefore could make such loans. NINJA loans were given to pretty much anybody that a decent credit score i.e. they were not delinquent in their credit history. Hence, if a person had just migrated from another country and had no job, no income and no assets, they could qualify for a mortgage! Even people who just got their credit scores immediately got a mortgage! Stories of people working menial jobs and having multiple homes were not uncommon during this era.

Although the lending standards were severely compromised in these types of loans, the market still had some innovations left. In the next discussion we shall have a closer look at two of the most important such innovations. They were important because they changed the very nature of the housing market.

Mortgage Products - Negative Amortization & Home Equity Line of Credit

In the previous two discussions, we have studied the <u>different types of mortgages from the borrowers</u> as well as from the <u>lenders</u> point of view. In this discussion we will look at some products which were called the byproduct of financial innovation. At first these products were applauded as being solutions to many problems. However, later when the financial markets went bust, these products ended up aggravating the crisis. There are many such products. However, most of the products are complicated and would be difficult to explain here. **In this discussion, we will have a look at the two most commonly used out of these products i.e. negative amortization and home equity line of credit**.

Negative Amortization Loans

Perhaps the most dangerous financial innovation of the subprime lending was a mortgage product known as negative amortization. Colloquially it was also referred to as "step up" loan. This loan was designed keeping in mind the needs of "wannabe" borrowers. This means this loan was designed to lure people to bet on the rise of their future income and take out loans which they will not be able to manage in the future. Banks have denied these charges and state that the risks of the negative amortization loans were well stated. However, borrowers and critics feel otherwise. Let's have a closer look at this financial innovation.

- **Step up Loans:** From the consumer point of view, negative amortization loans were really simple. Instead of having to pay $100 over the entire 30 year lifetime of the loan, borrowers were willing to pay $70 in the first 5 years, and then step it up to $85 in the next 5 years and then $100 for the next 5 and finally $125 for the last 5 years.

  To many borrowers, it made intuitive sense to do so. They figured that their incomes are low at this point of time. However, as and when they spend more times in their jobs, their incomes will always rise and then they will be able to afford the monthly payments. This is how these loans were marketed to entice the borrowers to take mortgages which were beyond their means by conventional lending standards.

. **Payment Less than Interest:** The math behind these loans was far more complicated than was being marketed. As we learned earlier that in the amortization process almost 80% of the payments made during the first 5 years go towards paying interest costs. Hence the bank was only charging $70 when in fact the more interest due was $80. This created a dangerous situation in the first five years of these loans.

. **Increasing Principal:** Now, the balance $10 i.e. ($80 interest vs. $70 payment) was added back to the principal! This happened month on month and the borrowers without being aware of it were paying compound interest on top of compound interest. The principal would spiral out of control within the first few years. Hence, it was possible that you took a $1000 to begin with and after 5 years of making payments, the balance outstanding was $1300! This could qualify as predatory lending. However, the banks had made the terms clear. It is the borrowers who believed the flashy commercials rather than read the fine print on the mortgage papers.

- **Dangers of Negative Amortization:** As we can see from the above case, the negative amortization loan is an extremely dangerous working arrangement. A naïve person may not realize that they are actually under water even after making regular monthly payments for 5 years. Also, if the income does not move up as expected, the borrower experiences financial duress. Most of these loans end up in duress or being foreclosed by the banks.

Home Equity Line Of Credit

Another dangerous type of financial innovation propagated by the banks during the subprime mortgage crisis is called Home Equity Line of Credit or HELOC for short. This arrangement allows for an abundance of credit and encourages the unsuspecting borrower to resort to unsustainable financial behavior.

- **Revolving Line of Credit:** The home equity line of credit is a revolving line of credit against the amount of equity that you have in your home. Consider the case of a person who has a $100 home and a $60 mortgage on that home. They therefore have $40 equity in the house. The mortgage company would offer them a revolving line of credit which they could use in their day to day lives. Since this credit was backed by a security, the rates of interest were very low.

- **Home Used as a Credit Card:** The HELOC allowed people to use their homes as a credit card. They could borrow the money from a mortgage company and spend on non mortgage related stuff. Many borrowers used this line of credit to pay off their credit cards. They also used this line of credit to remodel the house, buy a vacation and a lot of other goods and services that did not need to be purchased. As a result a lot of these households found themselves going back into debt!

- **Dangers of HELOC:** HELOC may sound like a good financial advice for a person suffering from debt issues. It sure makes sense to pay 4% interest instead of 36% on the balance on your credit cards. However, a lot of people started misusing the HELOC and went further into debt. They paid down their credit cards using HELOC and then charged more on their credit cards anyways! Of course this is not the banks problem. However, it is a dangerous product and must be sparingly used if it all and that too with extreme caution.

Both Negative Amortization and HELOC were applauded as being cutting edge financial innovations. However, they have done more harm than good. When the subprime mortgage market went down, a lot of people lost their homes and their lives savings thanks to these products.

The New Mortgage Landscape

The process of taking out a mortgage and the people with whom borrowers interact may not have undergone much change according to the borrower's point of view. However, the same cannot be said about the lenders point of view. The business of mortgage lending has changed completely in the previous 30 years or so. Earlier, there used to be one bank performing a variety of functions when loans were made. However, in the previous years all that has changed. This discussion will describe the new financial landscape and contrast it with the old financial landscape.

The Old Mortgage Landscape

The old mortgage world was pretty simple. There was a person who needed money to buy a house and then there was an institution (usually a bank) that was willing to lend the money to buy that house. The borrower would make monthly repayments of the loan over the next few years and then the loan got settled one day.

This simple world had a problem. The problem was that if the bank gave a mortgage loan to one person, they could expect to be repaid in full only after 30 years or so. Hence, for the next 30 years a portion of that money would always remain locked. Hence, the bank will not have that money to make new loans. Therefore the amount of mortgage loans that a bank could make was limited. This was an impediment to the existing political climate which wanted more and more home ownership and therefore wanted the banks to make as many mortgages as possible.

To solve this problem the new financial landscape was created. The new landscape was far more complicated. On one side there was the borrower whereas on the other side instead of there being a single institution i.e. the bank, there came to be a team of institutions. This discussion will describe the new arrangement in detail.

Originator

The bank that made the actual mortgage loan came to be known as the originator. This is because they would not hold the mortgage on their books for very long. Instead, they would simply sell the mortgages at a discount to other institutions. The liability of the bank was then over and they would be flush with cash to make more loans! Hence, the problem of the old financial landscape could be solved using this new arrangement. However, this new arrangement required several different types of players. The roles of some of them have been listed in this discussion.

Mortgage Brokers

Since the originator of the loan was no longer required to hold the loan for the entire tenure, banks were not the only people that could offer mortgages. A number of individuals who could raise some capital joined the business of making mortgages. They were called mortgage brokers. They were essentially doing the same function as the banks. The only difference being that they were not as big as the banks or were not subject to the same amount of regulatory checks. As long as the borrowers complied with certain criteria, they were free to make their loans which they could later sell off to the secondary mortgage market. The mortgage brokers themselves were a part of the primary mortgage market.

Servicer

Since mortgages last for decades, they need to be serviced too. There are people that will be late on their monthly payments, the others will have queries about how the interest rates reset and so on. Hence, there is an organization required to answer these queries and perform the customer service and collections end of the business.

These tasks came to be performed by independent third party agencies called "mortgage servicers". They were in the service industry and therefore were not a part of the secondary or primary mortgage market. However, since they were formed after the decentralization of the functions of the banks, they are often referred to as being part of the secondary mortgage market.

Underwriters

The secondary mortgage markets are based on the role of the underwriters. They are pivotal for the secondary market to function efficiently. This is because they buy the mortgages from the primary market. Then they securitize these loans. This means that if they buy a $95 loan from the market, they will create 100 $1 securities and sell them against the $95 loan. By doing so, they make a $5 profit. However, they have to underwrite these securities i.e. they have to guarantee to some extent that these loans will be paid off in due course of time. The values of their guarantees are different. Based on the value of their guarantees as well as the loan mix underlying the securities, these securities are priced in the open market. The underwriters basically define the secondary mortgage markets and therefore are undoubtedly a part of the secondary mortgage markets.

Special Purpose Entities

The investment banks wanted to steer clear of the additional liability that mortgage defaults would produce. Hence for every issuance of securities, they would create a special purpose entity. The purpose of this entity was to buy the mortgage securities from the investment banks and sell them to investors. It needs to be noted that the special purpose entities were selling these securities and not the banks. Hence, the banks had limited liability in these transactions.

Credit Rating Agencies

As we mentioned earlier, the value of the securities is largely based on who is guaranteeing them. Now, how do the investors know whose guarantee is worth what? For this purpose, credit rating agencies started venturing into the mortgage business. These agencies would rate the creditworthiness of the various investment banks, quasi government agencies and other special agencies who were issuing securities. Based on the ratings issued by these agencies, the value of the bonds would change.

Investors

The investors are finally the people who buy these securities from the open market. They could be individuals like you and me. Alternatively, they could be pension funds, municipal funds, insurance companies and so on.

In essence these are the people that are lending money to the borrower. They give their money to the underwriter who then gives it to the bank who then gives it to the borrower. Everyone else is only an intermediary holding the money for some time and slicing and dicing the mortgages. The real transaction is between the investors and the borrower. Also, since there is an active market for these securities, these securities are highly liquid and investors can exchange them for cash in an instant!

In the last three decades or so, the business of mortgage underwent a complete transformation. From being liquidity strapped and a long term business, it became a fast moving dynamic business. However, the roots of this business model were flawed as we shall see in the next discussion.

The New Mortgage Landscape: Conflict of Interest

In the previous discussion, we understood the new mortgage landscape and how it came to redefine the lending business. We also saw how a single lender now came to be replaced with multiple entities each of who were performing one specific function required in the mortgage market. The financial alchemists at the investment banks came to believe that they had created the perfect financial system. The idea was to keep the risk spread out amongst multiple individuals.

However, as we shall see in this discussion, the system was not nearly as perfect as it seemed at that time. Instead it was riddled with imperfections and flaws. These flaws were being criticized by critics. However, the voices of these critics were not heard at that time. Later when the system came crumbling down, these flaws became apparent. In this discussion, we will list down some of the flaws of this system.

Conflict of Interest - Originator

The originators in a traditional loan environment were very cautious about whom they lend their money to, particularly in the case of a mortgage. This is because a mortgage was a long term loan which would last for decades. Hence, the lender should have sufficient trust in the borrower.

However, in this new age financial system, trust was not required. The originator did not hold the loan for more than a few days on their books. Hence they were not really lending their money for decades. They were actually lending their money for a week or so. If the borrower did not default in this time frame (which is impossible since no payments become due) then they could make a loan to pretty much anybody and suffer no consequences.

Hence, the originators had no reason to be conservative about their lending. Each year they would try to get as big a piece of the origination market as possible with little regards as to whom they are making this loan to.

Conflict Of Interest - Servicer

Just like the originator, the servicer had no real reason to do their job dutifully. They had time bound and service level agreement bound contracts. As long as they adhered to those contracts, they would be paid in full. Since they had no stake in the mortgages, they had no incentive to collect information that could help the banks predict default rates.

Conflict Of Interest - Underwriters

The underwriters were also at the center of conflict of interest debate. In essence they were guaranteeing the mortgages. However, the investment banks were creating shell companies and corporate structures to ensure that the liabilities of these mortgages never come upon them. They were creating special purpose entities which were guaranteeing these mortgages. These shell companies were limited liability companies and had no connection to the investment banks whatsoever. Hence there was actually no one guaranteeing the loans!

Conflict Of Interest - Credit Rating Agencies

One of the biggest conflicts of interest situations was created between the underwriters and the credit rating agencies. The credit rating agencies were central to the secondary mortgage market concept. It was based on the accuracy of their ratings that the market would function efficiently. If they were of the view that a particular underwriter was going to face a credit crunch, they were supposed to reflect that opinion in that rating. However, it would not make any business sense for them to do so. This is because the underwriter is the one that had appointed them in the first place and paid them to conduct the very analysis. Hence, giving the underwriter a bad rating would mean no repeat business and hence loss of revenue. However, if they always gave the underwriter a good credit rating that would mean loss of trust and therefore once again loss of business.

Therefore, credit rating agencies always stuck to the middle path. They would not give very glamorous ratings or very distressed ones. In this way they could maintain both their repeat business as well as their reputation.

Critics had seen this coming a long time ago. However, agencies denied the allegations stating that their analyses are accurate and reflect the true underlying position. However, once the business model fell apart, this conflict of interest became readily apparent and was heavily criticized by the media and the general population. Credit rating agencies like Moody's and Standard and Poor's had to orchestrate massive public relations campaigns in the aftermath to save their reputations.

Conclusion

The new business model had therefore not improved the mortgage business at all. In fact, it had ruined the business. This is because earlier banks i.e. informed lenders would make loans to credible borrowers.

Under the new system, all the institutions were mere intermediaries and had no interest in seeing the loan get paid off. Instead, the people making the loans were uninformed lenders in the securities market. They did not have the information required to judge the credibility of the loans. Instead, they were just making bets on the market. Also, the borrowers had purely speculative motives and very few of them were actually interested in the underlying house.

Thus, the new financial system which was riddled with conflicts of interest from the start to the end had created a massive casino out of the lending market.

New Age Financial Securities

The new age mortgage market was extremely unlike the old one. The old one used to work based on a simple mortgage contract between the borrower and the lender. However, in the previous few discussions, we read about how the system has completely changed. Instead of the bank holding the loan for its entire tenure, mortgage debt is now traded in open markets like shares and bonds. These secondary markets and the open trading of these debts requires the use of new age financial securities. The 1990's and the 2000's saw the invention of many such securities. **In this discussion, we will discuss the two most important types of these securities i.e. mortgage backed securities and credit default swaps.**

Mortgage Backed Securities

We already know that in the new age world, banks do not actually fund mortgages. Rather they are intermediaries who originate loans and then sell it in the secondary mortgage market. This is enabled by a security known as mortgage backed security (MBS).

A mortgage backed security is a security that is backed by a mortgage or a pool of mortgages. Now, this may sound like confusing financial jargon. However, in essence it is very simple. When the bank makes a loan it sells it someone in the secondary market. These people in the secondary market collect a wide variety of such loans and create a "pool" of such loans. This pool therefore derives its cash flow from the mortgage payments it receives on a monthly basis. The pool is therefore nothing but a large mortgage which is a collection of many small mortgages.

Now, the sell the rights to own small pieces of these cash flows to investors via securities called mortgage backed securities. Let's say that at the end of every month there are $100 accumulated in the mortgage pool and there are 100 securities outstanding then they will pay each of them $1 each. Thus, mortgage backed securities derive its cash flows from the mortgage pool. Since they are "backed" by mortgages i.e. derive their cash flow from mortgages, they are called mortgage backed securities. The mortgage backed security is therefore often referred to as a "pass through" structure. The job of the mortgage backed securities is to allow the cash flow of the mortgages to be redirected to the holders of these securities i.e. it allows the cash to pass through.

There are several kinds of mortgage backed securities available in the market. The most important distinction lies between agency mortgage backed securities and private label mortgage backed securities. The mortgage backed securities are issued by quasi government agencies like Freddie Mac, Fannie Mae and Ginnie Mar. On the other hand, the private label securities are issued by special purpose entities created by investment banks. The agency mortgage backed securities usually sell at a premium because they are considered to be more secure since they are guaranteed by the quasi government agencies. Any debt guaranteed by these agencies is implicitly guaranteed by the taxpayers of the United States. Private label mortgage backed securities on the other hand have private guarantees which may be valuable depending upon their credit ratings.

Credit Default Swaps

Another instrument used in the new age financial markets is called credit default swaps. Although this instrument is not directly related to the mortgages, they were often used to bet against investment banks issuing mortgages. This is complex derivative structure and needs to be understood with caution.

A credit default swap is a kind of insurance. Let's say that I have a belief that Lehman Brother's bank is issuing bad quality debt and that they are going to default on their debt. In this case, I can go to a company issuing credit default swaps, (say AIG) and pay AIG a premium every month. In the event of a default by Lehman Brother's AIG will make good my losses.

This is exactly like insurance except for one major difference. I do not hold the debt issued by Lehman Brothers in the first place! It is like me buying insurance on my neighbor's car. I do not own the car. However, I pay insurance premiums on it and in the event of a default I get reimbursed for the loss of his car! I hope you see the difference. If we remove the principle of insurable interest from the insurance contract it turns into pure speculation and that is exactly what happened in the event of a credit default swap.

In the aftermath of the financial crisis of 2008, credit default swaps faced critical reviews and public outrage. The reason behind this was the fact that these contracts were highly unregulated. These contracts were mostly sold by regulated agencies i.e. banks and insurance agencies. However, they were so new to the market that the regulation had not caught up with them i.e. there were no laws requiring reserve requirements for these contracts. Hence, banks and insurance agencies could go on selling these contracts without keeping any money in the bank for a rainy day fund in case they all came due.

The first catastrophe of the credit default swaps was the insurance company AIG. The company literally faced a run on their assets as claims piled up after the housing market went bust and almost all the issuers of debt defaulted.

Since then, credit default swaps have been brought under the purview of legislation. The government is making it mandatory for the data regarding credit default swaps to be published so that it can be compared with the rating given by the rating agency and the true risk of the investment can be ascertained.

Collateralized Debt Obligations and Tranching

In the previous discussion, we learned about <u>mortgage backed securities</u>. We learned about how mortgages are pooled and then a special purpose entity is created as a pass through vehicle which allows security holders in the market to fund home owners to buy their homes.

However, in the case of mortgage backed securities, the cash flow from every security was identical in case it belonged to the same issuing entity. Therefore, all the securities from the same pool were fungible i.e. identical and could be exchanged for one another.

However, **the needs of the financial market led the creative investment bankers to build further on these ideas. This was the birth of what we now know as collateralized debt obligations (CDO's).** In this discussion, we will trace the evolution of the collateralized debt obligations (CDO's).

Different Needs

The mortgage backed securities only catered to the needs of the average investor. The mortgage risk was considered to be an average risk at that time. Therefore the mortgage backed securities were not fit for the needs of extremely risk averse investors such as pension funds. Pension funds would like to invest in mortgage backed securities only if they had a little less risk. They would not mind if the yield of the securities were compromised too. On the other end of the spectrum there were investors who wanted to take on high risks if the returns were good enough. Hedge funds and other private funds would fall into this category. Once again, the mortgage backed securities did not meet their needs. They were ready to buy these securities if they offered better return and did not mind taking the additional risk. So, the investment bankers observed that they were catering to the needs of only one type of investors. With the amount of mortgages they were buying, it would be difficult to securitize and sell them off unless they were also catering to the needs of the other two segments. Hence, a new instrument called collateralized debt obligations (CDO's) was born.

Same Pool Sliced Differently

The logic behind the collateralized debt obligations (CDO's) is simple. Instead of slicing the entire mortgage pool into similar pieces with the same risk return profile, they could slice the mortgage pool and create at least 3 different kinds of securities that would cater to the needs of these three different types of investors.

Hence, in case of collateralized debt obligations (CDO's), the process remains the same till the half way mark. The originator makes a loan, sells it to an investment bank, who then moves it into a special purpose entity. Only the last step is different. Here, is where the mortgages are sliced and securities are created.

At this stage, the investment bank does what has come to be known as tranching. Tranche is a French word which means slice. Hence, the investment bank is slicing the mortgages to create different types of securities. The most common way was to create three types of tranches.

- **Equity Tranche:** The bottom-most layer was called the equity tranche. If any defaults happened within the mortgage pool, they were first absorbed by the equity tranche. This meant that if any defaults happened they would not be split evenly amongst all the holders of the securities. Rather, the first blows will be taken by the people holding securities belonging to this tranche. Hence, they were facing an abnormally high risk of default as compared to members of the other tranches. As a result, they demanded more compensation. Therefore the equity tranche of the CDO's were for investors with a high risk high return profile. Hedge funds and the other investors were happy to buy these securities as they met their needs.

- **Mezzanine Tranche:** The middle layer was called the mezzanine tranche. The mezzanine tranche would remain unaffected by the defaults unless the value of the equity tranche was completely eroded. Once again the losses were not evenly split. The mezzanine tranche was second in the line of facing losses. Since they were relatively protected from these losses, they would get a lower return as compared to the people holding equity tranche securities from the same mortgage pool. The average investors who had an appetite for medium risk medium return profiles were happy to buy these securities.

- **Senior Tranche:** Finally, the top most layer was called the senior tranche. The senior tranche would remain unaffected from any losses until the value of the equity and mezzanine tranches was completely eroded. Since senior tranche securities were only a very small part of any issue, the likelihood of that happening was very minimal. Hence, these securities would enjoy a very good credit rating from the agencies. This made these extremely low risk and low return profile. As a result, they became viable investment options for ultra conservative investors like pension funds and sovereign funds.

Hence CDO's were able to help the mortgage backed securities proliferate every corner of the securities market. No matter what the risk return profile of the buyer, the securities market always had something to sell. In fact, CDO's became wildly popular in the years to come. There were even more innovations such as CDO square and CDO cube which were nothing but CDO's which were created out of a pool of another CDO's.

Benefits of Collateralized Debt Obligation (CDO's)

In the previous discussion, we studied about the beginning of the <u>collateralized debt obligations (CDO's)</u> and how they were born out of the mortgage backed securities. We also saw that collateralized debt obligations (CDO's) were not a way to magically get rid of risks. Instead, **these securities would ensure that everyone is not forced to take the risks**. They would just reassign the risks to whoever is willing to take them for a price. A lot of negative information about the collateralized debt obligations (CDO's) has been heard in the media. However, there are some positives to the story as well. We will look at the benefits in this discussion.

Catering To Different Investor Groups

The financial markets are full of investors with different kinds of needs. There are young single people and then there are grandpas. There are people who can afford to lose money and then there are people who wouldn't want to afford a single penny. Most asset classes can only cater to one or few of these investor groups. For instance equity is for the high risk investor whereas debt is for the low risk investor. However, that was not the case with mortgages after collateralized debt obligations (CDO's) were introduced. Collateralized debt obligations (CDO's) were the miracle of structured finance which allowed the same product to be sold to multiple sellers who had very different risk reward needs. This created a huge demand for these securities which was desirable because selling a large number of these securities would help society pursue the American dream of owning a house.

Flexible Tenures

Mortgage loans were known for being highly illiquid as well as for having very large tenures. A typical mortgage loan would last for three decades. Most investors were not willing to buy securities with such a long maturity even if there was an active secondary mortgage market for them to cash out and leave. This is because the cash flows that will arise from these mortgages three decades hence are impossible to predict even for the most sophisticated of investors. It is for this reason that collateralized debt obligations (CDO's) became more popular. Through the use of the tranching technique it was possible to create multiple securities with shorter or longer tenures as required by the buyers. This also led to the proliferation of collateralized debt obligations (CDO's) since these securities could literally be custom made to meet the needs of the clients.

Overcollateralization

One of the biggest risks facing the buyers of any kinds of bonds is the risk of prepayment. In case there is a prepayment there are left with the principal and no way to invest it at the same rate of return. This was even more common in the mortgage markets since many mortgages were being taken out for purely speculative purposes. Hence, at least a portion of them were to repaid within the first few years. To counter this problem, the investment bankers started using a process called overcollateralization while creating the collateralized debt obligations (CDO's). Hence, if they had mortgages worth $200, they would sell bonds only for $150. The balance $50 would act as a buffer to absorb prepayments and hence the name overcollateralization. However, once prepayments crossed the $50 mark, they would have to be absorbed by the bondholders depending upon which tranche they belong to. However, under normal circumstances the likelihood of that happening was minimal. Once again the collateralized debt obligations (CDO's) were made more marketable by the use of this practice.

Principal Only Bonds

There was a class of investors that was still wary that the homeowners would decide to refinance and prepay their debts at the exact moment when the interest rates were low. This would leave the bondholders with a pile of cash and no way to invest it at a high interest rate. To cater to the needs of such people, the makers of collateralized debt obligations (CDO's) created a different class of security called the principal only bond. This was very similar to the zero coupon bond in the fact that it sold at a discount and then it would be retired for its full value on maturity. Hence, the holders of these bonds would receive their money at an earlier time ensuring that the time weighted return on their investment would be higher than it would otherwise have been. Principal only bonds were preferred by the more senior and the more conservative investors.

Interest Only Bonds

The opposite of principle only bonds were interest only bonds. These bonds were meant for the risky investors since their value could dramatically change virtually overnight. In case of a prepayment, the borrower need not make any more interest payments. Hence, the holders of interest only bonds will get paid drastically less if the interest rates fall and a lot of borrowers decide to refinance their homes or pay the amount upfront. The converse of this was also true, in case of no prepayments the holders of these bonds would get paid a lot and for a long time and would end up making a killing! Hence, the collateralized debt obligations (CDO's) were structured in such a way that the high risk investors could also get a piece of the pie.

These benefits of the collateralized debt obligations (CDO's) were well known at the time. This is why these instruments were considered to be the creation of brilliant innovative minds. However, lesser known was the fact that mortgage payments and interest rates were highly sensitive and difficult to predict. Therefore, no matter how sophisticated an investor is they simply did not have the means to find out what these securities were worth.

Subprime Crisis: Problems Caused by Accounting

The subprime mortgage crisis was caused by a myriad of factors coming together. There was faulty lending, speculative borrowing, there was an ill conceived secondary mortgage market and then there was also the wrong accounting techniques being used. In this discussion we will focus on the problems with the accounting used by the firms in the subprime mortgage crisis. It is important to note that the crisis was not an accounting fraud. This means that the books were not cooked and the numbers were not made up. All the accounting techniques used were perfectly legal. They were legal yet flawed.

However, the accounting techniques did magnify the crisis once it happened. **The accounting technique which was brought into question by the critics is called mark to market accounting**. We will discuss the pitfalls of the same and how it related to the subprime mortgage crisis in this video.

Mark to Market Accounting

It is important to note that this is not the first time that mark to market accounting is being criticized. It has always been considered to be a very aggressive accounting method. Nobel Prize winning economist Milton Friedman has criticized it severely on many occasions. Also, this method was blamed in the biggest accounting fraud in Corporate America i.e. Enron Inc.

Let's briefly understand how mark to market accounting works. Usually when an investment is purchased it is recorded in the balance sheet at cost price. This cost price remains the same on the balance sheet regardless of what the market value of these assets is. The market value is recorded as a gain or loss only when the asset is sold. For instance, if I buy a security for $100, it reflects on my balance sheet as $100 even if its market value is $130. Only when I sell the security for $130 does the $30 gain get recorded. As long as it is on the balance sheet no gain or loss is recorded.

In the case of mark to market accounting, this is not the case. Gains and losses are immediately recognized and booked to the profit and loss account. Hence in our example, if we purchase the security for $100 and its value changes to $130, we mark these securities to market. This means that we recognize $30 of additional gain. Remember that no transaction has taken place and this gain is purely fictional. The firm does not have this additional $30 to justify the entry. However, this is how mark to market works and this is what perpetuated the subprime mortgage crisis cycle.

The Upward Spiral

Now, the **subprime mortgage saw both the upside and the downside of the mark to market accounting**. Let's see the upside first. During the borrowing boom, home prices were rising, interest rates were falling and there were almost no defaults. Hence, the securities purchased by investors or held by investment banks for trading were rising in value. In many cases, they were rising at double the rate of the other securities because of the perceived financial innovation. In these heydays, the companies holding these securities were constantly recognizing the gain in the profit and loss accounts. This gave unwary investors the picture that the company is earning record profits. This made their stocks trade at higher multiples and made the company appear more valuable than it really was!

Hence, the mark to market accounting did not create the subprime boom in the first place but rather perpetuated it. It allowed companies to recognize fictional gains and created a stock market boom which was completely based on the boom of the mortgage securities market!

The Downward Spiral

The downward spiral was much more painful for the companies involved. This is because just like the gains, the losses also have to be marked to market on an immediate basis. Hence if the value of $100 security falls to $80, the company is required by accounting standards to immediately recognize the $20 loss. This proved very costly on the fateful day that Lehman brothers fell.

On the day that Lehman Brothers collapsed, the mortgage securities market took a nosedive in valuation. Many of the securities which were highly valued were now being valued at close to zero. As a result of this all the investment banks and investors that were heavily invested in these securities had to take an immediate write down in the valuations. Now, it needs to be understood that these securities were not sold yet and the value of these balance sheets remained uncertain. However, there was an immediate write down. As a result, the balance sheets of many of these companies started appearing to be unhealthy. Therefore there was a massive panic and sell off in the stock markets. What started as a bust in the mortgage market quickly threatened the existence of the global financial system.

Once again, mark to market accounting did not cause the catastrophe. However, it aggravated the downside by magnifying it.

Conclusion

Mark to market accounting is a dangerous accounting policy. It must be used very carefully and with caution. Even more so when it is being used to account for speculative securities like the ones that were being used in the mortgage markets. The subprime mortgage mess ended with severe discussions on mark to market accounting as well as curtailing its widespread usage.

The Self Reinforcing Housing Loop

The subprime mortgage crisis was undeniably an asset bubble. The fundamentals had not changed on the ground. The people had not started making twice as much money as they were making earlier. Neither had the price for constructing the houses fallen by half. However, still the prices of houses across the United States doubled in a very short period of time. This rise in prices was way above the usual rise and had no basis to support it. In this discussion, we will have a closer look as to how the economy reached this position wherein the market could turn into an unsustainable bubble.

We will look at the subprime mortgage crisis through the lens of the asset bubble theory and make an attempt to identify the feedback loops that were operational.

Low Interest Rates

The entire process started when the US government cut the interest rates to 1.75%. Interest forms a huge part of the mortgage payments. So much so that in the first 5 years or so 75% of the payments made go towards interest charges. Hence, slashing the interest rates to a fourth of what they were resulted in the first step of the asset bubble. For any asset bubble to arise there has to be easy access to a lot of money. When the Fed cut the lending rates, it literally pumped it billions of dollars in the market and with the political motives surrounding home ownership, the biggest chunk of this newly created money ended up in the mortgage markets. The common denominator amongst all asset bubbles in the recent past has been extended periods of low interest rates.

Speculative Activity

This excess money in the market caused the people to indulge in speculative activity. Historically, for the last five decades, the United States had witnessed a steady rise in housing prices. Housing prices would increase at the rate of inflation. Hence, when money was in abundance, inflation was bound to be high. A high inflation combined with a low interest rate meant that anybody who could get a mortgage would end up making a big profit on their investment. This is because the mortgages are highly leveraged and even a small movement in the price creates a big change in return.

Also, since the construction industry is the second largest employer in the country, the housing boom was seen as a good thing. However, most of the new houses being built were out of the city areas and as many as 22% of the houses were vacation homes and a large portion of them were second homes. The people holding these 30 year mortgages had no intention of holding them till the end, most wanted to make a quick buck and move on. Hence, the low interest rates had created the first stage of the bubble i.e. the boom.

Secondary Mortgage Markets

Low interest rates had unleashed a lot of money into the market. However, even a lot of money would have quickly dried up with the amount of loans that were being made. That did not happen because the US investment banks had found a way to recycle the same money over and over again. They spent the 1990's and 2000's perfecting the secondary mortgage markets. Thus banks did not have to hold on their investments till the end of the mortgage. Rather within a couple of weeks, the funds would be recycled and banks would be flush with cash to make more and more loans. The secondary markets took a majority of the blame for the crash. However, they were only a small reason behind the crisis.

More Speculation

The speculators described in point number 2 above ended up making some serious money on their investments. The success of the speculators did not go unnoticed by the media and the community at large. Many of these speculators further reinvested their earnings into the housing market buying multiple houses giving rise to even more speculation. Moreover, seeing the success of the early movers, even the average guy started plunging into debt to enter the mortgage market. This debt binge was made possible by the availability of easy loans. However, the temporary success of many peers seemed to be the catalyst. At this point in time, the fundamentals had begun to deviate from the reality. There were young people, insolvent people and jobless people who had houses and had no idea how they were going to pay off the mortgage. They also had no intention of holding on to the mortgage. The housing market had become the new stock market. In an ideal scenario the market would have went bust by now. However, the extended period for which the interest rates were held low as well as the secondary mortgage markets made it possible for the bubble to inflate further.

Unsustainable Conditions

The last three to four years before 2008, were like the beginning of the end of the Ponzi scheme that the United States housing market had become. Housing prices had doubled in tripled in most parts of the country in the last six years or so. **If anyone had any money there was only one place they wanted to invest that is the housing market.**

Couple this with the fact that no money was required to buy a house and an unsustainable boom emerges. Cases of bartenders with multiple homes and immigrant workers with beach houses were not uncommon during this period. The fundamentals had deviated too far from what was the reality.

The reality was that these mortgages could not be paid off and that it was only a matter of time before the system fell apart. Many people had seen this coming and made a lot of money predicting the failure of these banks. However, if anyone had been paying attention to the asset bubble theory they could have easily predicted the market bust.

Integrated Financial Systems: Boon or Bane

The subprime mortgage meltdown has raised many questions in the markets. Most of them have been unpleasant and most of them have been about things which we earlier thought were good and which are now viewed in a negative light. One such issue is the issue of integrated financial markets. The subprime mortgage crisis is supposed to be a very local crisis in scope. It is a crisis of the real estate industry in the United States i.e. one industry in one nation. However, it turns out that this crisis metamorphosed into a catastrophe. All markets all over the world were affected by the impact of this crisis and the result was a global recession. This brings to the fore the extreme connectedness of the markets in the world today. **In this discussion, we will have a closer look at the connections between these markets and how they affected the subprime mortgage meltdown**.

Mortgage Markets and Bond Markets

As we have already discussed in previous discussions, the very nature of mortgage products was changed. Banks were no longer the ones supplying the money to the homeowners to buy the mortgage. Instead, it was the people in the bond market who were doing so. The banks were just a pass through vehicle to facilitate the meeting of these two counterparties.

With the advent of the quasi government agencies, big chunks of mortgages started to be securitized and be sold in the bond market. These agencies had the backing of the government and were therefore able to make stellar profits out of these transactions. This attracted Wall Street and its brand of subprime and Alt A mortgage backed securities to the bond market too. Towards the end of the crisis, pretty much every mortgage loan made in the United States found its way into the bond markets. The volumes of these bonds were so high that they formed the majority of bonds being traded in the market.

Hence, it would be safe to say that mass securitization linked the fate of bind markets and mortgage markets together. A change in any of these markets was certain to affect the functioning of the other one.

Bond Markets and Stock Markets

Just like the mortgage markets, the stock future of the stock markets was also inexorably linked with the bond markets. Most of the companies selling these mortgage backed securities and collateralized debt obligations were listed on the stock exchange. This includes all Wall Street Investment Banks as well as quasi government agencies like Freddie Mac, Fannie Mae and Ginnie Mae. Real estate was the dominant investment theme in those days. Hence investors looking for an indirect exposure to the sector were also heavily invested in these stocks. This coupled with the fact that mark to marked accounting allowed all these firms to post sky high profits was also responsible for bringing about a stock market boom which was driven by the mortgage and bond markets.

Hence, another level of financial integration was inadvertently reached. The bond markets and the stock markets were linked together in a manner that both would move in tandem and more often than not this movement was caused by the mortgage market!

Bond Markets and Derivative Markets

Another very important linkage is the one between the bond market and the derivatives market. As we are aware that most of the financial instruments being sold over the counter in the mortgage markets also had derivative counterparts. For instance collateralized debt obligations and credit default swaps were the famous derivatives products being sold. The volume of trade in the mortgage market had exploded and so had the volume of trade in the linked derivatives market. The number of securities and contracts outstanding was simply astounding. In fact they were enough to bring erstwhile financial behemoths to their knees. And a large number of these contracts were either directly based on the mortgage markets or were based on the bonds and stocks that were mimicking the mortgage markets.

Hence, along with the stock and bond markets, the derivative markets were also linked to the mortgage market creating a scenario wherein every major market in the United States would move in correlation.

Local Markets and Foreign Markets

To add to the above fact, the securities based on subprime mortgage loans were not based in the US only. Rather investors all the world had developed an appetite for them. It is for this reason that pension and municipality funds from far off places like Europe were rapidly making its way into the subprime securities. Some municipalities like the Municipality of Dusseldorf were heavily invested in these mortgages. Therefore, there was a situation where in a slight movement in the mortgage markets could send shockwaves all over the United States and even overseas!

This was not the case, a couple of decades earlier. The markets were fairly independent of one another.

However, the new age financial innovation led to an inadvertent consequence of sewing these markets together!

This was one of the ingredients in the final bust of 2008. What should ideally have been a local crisis became an international crisis threatening the financial system! This brings us to the question as to whether linking together of the financial markets is a good thing? Sure, it can provide convenience in the short run. However, it also leads to the correlation of all the markets. Therefore everything goes through the boom bust cycle simultaneously causing the massive shockwaves.

Credit Market Freeze - Causes and its Importance

The sub-prime mortgage crisis and the credit freeze are often spoken about in the same breath. In fact, the layman would believe that both these words actually refer to the same event. However, that is not the truth. The subprime mortgage crisis played out in the bond markets whereas the credit freeze played out in the interbank lending markets. They two may have been related. However, both of them are mutually exclusive events. In the <u>previous discussions</u>, we have studied all about the subprime mortgage crisis. **In this discussion, we will look at the details of what caused the credit freeze and why was it important ?**

Interbank Markets

Banks are required to maintain a certain amount of reserves on hand with the Central Bank. In return, the Central Bank is required to bail out individual banks as well as the banking system in case of unforeseen events like a run on the banks.

However, as the banks conduct their business of day to day borrowing and lending, it is unlikely that they will always have the exact number to meet the reserve requirements. The banking system as a whole will have the exact reserve requirements. However, individual banks may not have the requisite amount of reserves. Hence banks trade reserves with each other in a market known as the interbank market.

As the name suggests, this is basically a market where banks make unsecured loans to other banks. The tenure of these loans varies from overnight to a few days. This market is the backbone of the modern fractional reserve banking system and any issues in the interbank markets always have large scale implications. This was the case with the credit freeze of 2008.

Uncertainty Post Lehman Brothers

The interbank lending market is made up of banks that are willing to lend to other banks. The lending is primarily unsecured. This means in case of Bank A making a bad loan to Bank B and bank B collapsing, Bank A simply has to write down the loans given in the interbank market i.e. they do not have any recourse.

In 2008, the days after the fall of Lehman Brothers fall, there was a credit freeze. The reason behind this is simple. Lehman Brothers was a massive bank and had dealings with all other banks in the United States and across the world. Hence, when Lehman Brothers collapsed, all the firms that were left holding Lehman's debt were not going to be paid. There was therefore increasing suspicion amongst the banking community regarding lending to other banks. What if the other bank held a significant amount of Lehman debt and was never going to be paid? What if the other bank collapsed? Hence, the Lehman Brothers collapse brought about a situation wherein banks were simply not lending to other banks in the interbank market. They were uncertain about the balance sheets of the other banks and knew that they would end up undertaking excessive risk. Since no one was lending credit and liquidity all over the world froze.

The Effect of the Freeze

The effect of the freeze on the banking system was catastrophic. Firstly, it became known to the public that the banking system was in jeopardy. The bankers did not trust each other, so then how could they expect the individuals to trust them with their money. As a result, there were old fashioned runs on the bank and some institutions were simply bankrupted.

Apart from that, the banks were unable to find enough liquidity for their functioning. Unless they were able to generate more funds, their loan making capabilities were hindered. Usually, they would just borrow the shortfall from the interbank market. However, of late the interbank markets had simply frozen.

Central Banks Intervene

It took central bank intervention to break this standoff credit freeze between the member banks. The European Central Bank and the Federal Reserve realized the gravity of the situation. They also understood that unless action was immediately taken, more problems would arise.

As a result, the Central Bank of Europe pumped billions of euros into the interbank market on its own. When banks were not willing to lend to one another, the Central Bank was willing to take the risk on its member banks. Seeing the situation stabilize in Europe, the Federal Reserve also followed suit and pumped in billions of dollars into the US interbank market. Once again, the Fed was willing to take the counterparty risk. As a result of this intervention, the credit freeze was eliminated.

The Fed and European Central Bank had succeeded in temporarily kick-starting the market. However, they did not want to be making loans in the long run. In the long run, they wanted the banks to be lending out money to each other. Therefore to induce this behavior and end the credit freeze, the Fed and the ECB cut the repo rate by a few basis points. As a result, the banks started lending out money to other member banks.

Systemic Risks

The credit freeze of 2008 brought to light the systemic risk faced by the entire financial world. If the crisis had been a little bit more grave and the Central Banks, a little less prepared, the world would have seen a much bigger financial disaster. Since the 2008 crisis was mitigated, major banking regulators of the world are trying to create a system in which such a credit freeze scenario never plays out again.

Mortgage Lending: Borrower Approach vs Collateral Approach

The subprime mortgage crisis was basically a clash of ideologies. These ideologies were related to the centuries old belief regarding how money should be lent out versus the new age beliefs regarding how money should be lent out. **The old age belief was that money is being lent out to the borrower and that collateral should be set aside and the borrower's ability to pay back should be taken into account.**

In this discussion we will have a closer look at the clash between the two approaches.

The Borrower Approach

The borrower approach was based on centuries of sound lending practices. This is how money had always been lent out. Some of the maxims of this old age approach have been listed below:

- **Ability to Pay:** The old age lending technique was very skeptical about the borrower's ability to pay back the loan that they were asking for. The assumption would be that the borrower will not be able to pay back and the documentation would be used to create a case otherwise. Each document was looked at with extreme skepticism. Detailed analyses of what the borrower's cash flows would look like in the future were drawn out. There were heuristics which governed the amount of money that the borrower must pay towards the mortgage in case they were to maintain their lifestyle and not face any liquidity crunch.

The new age lending analysis simply discounted the borrower and the old adage. They simply believed that it was the borrower's job to look at their budget and not the bank's. The bank was lending against collateral i.e. a house and if the borrower failed to pay back the money, well they would simply foreclose the house and obtain their money!

- **Willingness to Pay:** The old age lending took a very close look at the borrower's willingness to pay the debts besides the borrower's ability to do so. This was done by closely scrutinizing the past debts that were held by the borrower. Were they paid back on time? Did the borrower follow the repayment schedule or was there a delay in making the payments? Did the borrower have any incidences of bankruptcies or foreclosures?

The new age lending has a much better mechanism to keep a track record of all the above questions. This mechanism is called the "credit score" and it aggregates all the above questions into one easy to understand number. However, competition between the new age bankers led them to believe that this number was not as important as it seemed to be. The rationale once again was the same. The transaction is secured with a house of greater value and hence they shouldn't really be worrying about all these things.

- **Stress Testing:** The old age lending was conservative in the valuation of properties. The definitely did not believe in the maxim that property prices will always appreciate. Hence they would always ask for down payments that would act as a cushion in case the price of the property fluctuated. Mortgages after all lasts for about three decades on an average and a lot can change regarding the valuation of the property in that time frame. Also, the lenders would assume what would happen if distressful scenarios such as divorce, illness or any other expense were to come the borrower's way. Only if the borrower's outlook was positive in all of these scenarios were the loans made.

The new age lending practice was the exact opposite of this. Down payments were reduced to a minimum. Also, there were soft second loans available to help borrowers make the margin payment. Therefore in essence the bank was financing 100% of the property instead of 80%. No attention was paid to any duress that the borrower may face in their lives.

Problems with the Collateral Approach

The collateral approach to lending had some major flaws. These flaws were what later caused the subprime debacle. Two of the most prominent flaws in this approach have been listed down below:

- **Illiquid:** It is true that the bank did have a claim to a property in the event of a default. However, it is not true that the bank should not worry about borrowers defaulting. A default scenario is a no win scenario. In fact it is a lose-lose scenario if the defaults happen in mass. This is because properties are not like stocks and bonds, they cannot be sold overnight. In fact property investments can take months to liquidate. On top of that there are legal expenses and transaction costs that need to be borne by the banks too. Hence, if the borrower defaults the bank is stuck with a property. But the banks are not in the business of leasing properties. Instead they are in the business of lending out money and it takes a long time to convert the property into money!

- **Volatile Value:** The nail in the coffin of the new age approach is that houses also have volatile value. This is particularly true in the case when lending standards have been extremely relaxed and when defaults happen in mass. When everybody wants to sell their homes there is excess supply and no demand causing the prices to plunge. In the absence of any margin money, banks literally have to write off millions of dollars in losses. This is precisely what happened as result of the subprime mortgage crisis.

The bottom line therefore is that collateral is meant to make lending easier. It is not the sole purpose of lending. The age old maxim still holds true. Loans are still made to borrowers and a thorough credit check is the only way to ensure sustainable profitable lending.